# BASS RE

# THE LONE RANGER:

## Debunking the Myth

by Martin Grams, Jr.

© 2018, OTR Publishing, LLC

Readers can spot the difference between historical writing and artistic imagination, even if they cannot explain the difference between them. A good historian begins with chronology, crafts the biography, and sprinkles anecdotes throughout. The best historians are known for consulting historical archives and presenting only the facts, but perhaps the toughest undertaking is deciding what to leave out. Ever careful in their research, historians attempt to present accurate history after carefully weighing the available evidence. Historians are expected to present only the facts to avoid spawning rumors, misconceptions and myths that ultimately take decades to debunk. One such example is a misconception about the exploits of an African-American U.S. Deputy Marshal named Bass Reeves, triggered by recent folklore influenced by racial bias brought about by false beliefs and a genuine lack of concern for factual verification. Besides documenting the true accomplishments of Reeves, a book published a decade ago caused unnecessary confusion by falsely suggesting he was the inspiration for the fictional character of *The Lone Ranger*. Historians are expected to avoid the pitfall of mistaking folklore for facts, in large measure through the avoidance of speculations. However, the author of the Bass Reeves biography ultimately – and unintentionally – misled tens of thousands of readers into believing a falsehood.

A number of recently-published books about Bass Reeves have increased popularity for the historic figure. His career was extensively – and impressively – documented in *Black Gun, Silver Star: The Life and Legend of Frontier Marshal Bass Reeves*, published in 2006 by University of Nebraska Press. The author, Art T. Burton, consulted census records and a large number of second-hand accounts, reflections and insights to compile a 346-page tome documenting the life and career of Bass Reeves. "Much of what we know today about Bass Reeves persisted in oral stories told by individuals and families whose origins are in frontier Oklahoma" (Burton 11). The author devoted much of the first chapter of his book reprinting numerous recollections from people who never met Reeves personally, documenting facets of Reeves's life as it was passed down to them from someone who claimed to have met the lawman. The author admits in his book that the majority of people who personally knew Reeves had passed on, so the stories reported in the book could never stand the standard scrutiny of historians who are diligent in separating fact from fancy, or reality from rumor. The entire book, with the exception of the first chapter, was properly researched according to accepted historian practices.

Among Burton's suggestive claims in that first chapter was that the fictional *Lone Ranger*, a radio and television property that gained popularity through sponsorship and mass merchandising starting in the 1930s, was based on the historic exploits of Bass Reeves. Through carefully-selected wording Burton assured readers that his statements were merely theories, with no facts on which to base his conclusion. Failing to follow proper guidelines such as the avoidance of printed speculation, Burton ultimately created a modern-day myth of interminable proportions. Casual readers overlooked the precise and nuanced wording that Burton employed, and were led to a false impression regarding the facts. As a result, it is estimated that over 100 blogs and websites on the Internet today are reprinting the false connection between Bass Reeves and *The Lone Ranger*, with many going so far as to report the story as factual. This essay will debunk and verify, through evidence and historical documents, that Bass Reeves was never the inspiration for *The Lone Ranger*. With a historian's motivation to set the record straight and hopefully stop the spread of this myth on the Internet, this essay will disprove Art T. Burton's theory.

Relatively un-researched and undocumented for many decades, black frontiersmen have recently become the substance of published reference guides. With publishing companies recognizing greater interest in African-American history and biography, even with topics that might seem obscure to the mainstream public, more books have been published in the last decade about black frontiersmen than decades prior. Print-on-demand technology has opened the door to independent publishing, making it easier for research materials to reach a public hungry for more books of the like. Leading up to the theatrical release of *The Lone Ranger* in 2013, produced by The Walt Disney Company, Jerry Bruckheimer and Johnny Depp's Infinitum Nihil production company, Burton's claim that Bass Reeves might have been the inspiration for *The Lone Ranger* reached the news media and numerous bloggers. Word spread like wildfire on the Internet regarding what appeared to be an injustice to Bass Reeves. Blogs and websites with an economic rather than academic agenda failed to verify the facts before they went to print and ran with the story. Blogs and websites providing a platform for feedback gave readers an opportunity to voice their opinions. This, in part, detracted from the good name of Bass Reeves as readers focused not on his exploits and accomplishments, but instead on the fake *Lone Ranger* connection for which readers were primarily fixated.

Bass Reeves was inspired by his father, who served in district law as the county sheriff and tax collector, to become a Deputy U.S. Marshal. Motivated by the difficulties of racial intolerance in the regions of Texas and Oklahoma it was Reeves's intent to earn respect among a community comprised generally of white men and American Indians. Through second-hand accounts collected in Burton's book, it is believed that Reeves possessed superb tracking skills and notoriety for being a sharp-shooter. Among the many myths of the Bass Reeves's lore was his legendary physical strength, described as "superhuman" (Burton 16). Burton's biography accurately depicts Reeves's accomplishments through testimony in court records and painted a portrait of a larger-than-life hero of the western frontier. It is the first chapter in Burton's book that provided five specific "coincidences" in what the author claimed was a direct connection to *The Lone Ranger*.

The first of these five was Burton's contention that Reeves worked in disguise in an effort to get close enough to fugitives to apprehend them. To claim this component of Reeves's career could have inspired the script writers of *The Lone Ranger* to wear a mask and disguise is a stretch. Masked vigilantes were commonplace among pulp fiction, from Johnston McCulley's Zorro in *The Curse of Capistrano* (1919) and Russell Thorndike's Dr. Christopher Syn, alias the Scarecrow (circa 1915), to *The Shadow* (beginning in 1931) and the daring adventures of Robin Hood. Surely those fictional characters, among hundreds of others, were not all inspired by the escapades of Bass Reeves on the basis of his disguise?

Burton claims that Reeves, when he ventured into uncharted territory, was accompanied by an Indian guide. "Federal law mandated that deputy U.S. marshals had at least one posseman with them whenever they went out in the field" (Burton 11). Pioneers, hunters and bounty hunters commonly took along an Indian colleague for both protection and as a guide. Overlooking this fact, Burton suggested that the creation of Tonto, the fictional and faithful Indian sidekick for *The Lone Ranger*, was one of five reasons why Bass Reeves was the inspiration for *The Lone Ranger* radio program.

In one account, he related that Reeves, while hunting down members of the Dalton gang, paid for his meal – and the meal of the possemen – with a silver dollar. "Before they went out on the hunt the posse ate breakfast and Reeves paid for the meal with a silver dollar …. We all know that the Lone Ranger's calling card was the silver bullet. Quite possibly Reeves's was the silver dollar" (Burton 13). How this one-time incident could be a unique trademark borrowed for use on *The Lone Ranger*, as suggested by Burton, remains unclear. At that time silver dollars were commonly used as a standard form of currency. The United States Mint produced dollar coins made of silver as early as 1794 and substantially increased production during the years 1836 to 1873.

Burton's strongest supporting statement to connect the two men was that "Reeves may have ridden a white horse during one period of his career" (Burton 13) and elaborated on his statement by describing an incident in which "witnesses testified that the cook threatened to shoot Reeves's gray horse. A gray horse can look anywhere from near black to near white, so it was possible that Reeves rode a horse that appeared to be white" (Burton 13). Over 100 breeds of horses and mustangs were used for military, farming and transportation during the 1800s, all varied in color from black, paint, gray and white. Reeves would have had more than one horse in his lifetime. Through Burton's own admission the color of Reeves's horse cannot be verified as white – another tenuous connection to *The Lone Ranger*.

Burton's claim of "another possible connection, though tenuous, is that the original story of the Lone Ranger began on the radio, in Detroit, in 1933. Many of the fugitives arrested by Bass Reeves and later convicted at Fort Smith, Arkansas, were sent to the Detroit House of Corrections in Michigan" (Burton 13). In his defense, Burton remarked on my blog, "The radio station was owned by a lawyer, George W. Trendle. Being a lawyer it is quite possible that Trendle talked to criminal justice attorneys in Detroit, especially as it related to the Detroit House of Corrections" (www.martingrams.blogspot.com). What Burton failed to acknowledge was that Trendle specialized in contract law, never criminal justice.

Because *The Lone Ranger* was of muscular build, had an Indian guide named Tonto as a sidekick, often wore a black mask to prevent his true identity from becoming known, used silver bullets as a trademark calling card, and rode a white stallion named Silver, Burton attempted to lay out a strong suggestive claim that *The Lone Ranger* was based on the daring exploits of Bass

Reeves. These points, along with the fact that *The Lone Ranger* radio program originated from radio station WXYZ in Detroit, Michigan, was the icing on Burton's case.

To debunk the myth academically involves clarifying several points. I plan to do this by:

First, verifying that every print publication making reference to a *Lone Ranger*-Bass Reeves connection and claim of comparison can be traced back to Burton's book. This is important because it indicates that no book, website or blog on the Internet claiming the comparison as fact was available prior to Burton's publication. Historical documents are being discovered constantly and historians are careful to note the use of historical references in works, constructing something similar to a family tree, to understand the validity of research.

Second, providing documentation of the origin and formation of *The Lone Ranger* radio program, for the benefit of verifying that the fictional character was established by a number of creative forces, residing in different states, disproving the theory that one person conspired against Bass Reeves and that one person was never solely responsible for the creation of *The Lone Ranger*, and that fictional literature including Zorro and Robin Hood were among the true inspirations.

Third, reminding readers that Burton never stated in his book conclusively that Bass Reeves was the inspiration for the fictional masked man, but used cautionary words to provide a theory based on mere coincidences.

One modern way of publishing research is the use of online blogs. As defined by Webster, "a blog is a website containing postings that open the door to commentary and discussion, but are not necessarily based on fact." One can see the ripple effects of the Burton book rather plainly by how often wording or cited numbers are repeated without question. According to Marshall Trimble on *True West Magazine*'s website, the deputy marshal "arrested more than 3,000 men and women without being wounded" (Trimble 1). That same number is featured among a number of other website blogs including Donna Klein of Recollections.biz, Kathy Weiser of Legendsofamerica.com, and Lt. Dan Marcou of Policeone.com.

A personal inquiry to each of these individuals, asking for their source of the specified number all yielded the same results. They saw this number on another blog or website. Further, Gaius Chamberlain of Greatblackheroes.com cited the same number and, when the source of his information was questioned, he mentioned the previously-referenced book by Art T. Burton.

The boundaries of formal and informal publication have been put to the test in the past decade. Scholars and historians prefer to avoid blurred lines and never take note of the information on any given website, but rather the sources. Wikipedia, always under scrutiny in the academic field, has methods in place for refuting or documenting new data, but those are crowdsourced without the systematic editing of an expert for any particular listing. Therefore, even the Wikipedia entry has no new research at the time of this writing, citing personal website blogs and unconfirmed websites that reference only the Burton work and no archival materials.

The name of Bass Reeves appears in relatively few printed reference guides prior to Burton's book; the earliest was published in 1971, almost forty years after the premiere of *The Lone Ranger* on radio. No books referencing the name Bass Reeves, other than those listed in Appendix A, have been found to predate Art T. Burton's biography. With but one exception, the common denominator among these reference guides is the exclusion of any reference to *The Lone Ranger* and/or a connection to Bass Reeves.

That one exception was John W. Ravage and his book *Black Pioneers: Images of the Black Experience on the Northern American Frontier*, asking the question, "Could Bass Reeves be the prototype for the Lone Ranger character?" (Ravage 66). The author posed the question with no supporting facts, providing only an offhanded and facetious comment for the amusement of his readers. Art T. Burton wrote in his book, "I doubt we would be able to prove conclusively that Reeves is the inspiration for *The Lone Ranger*. We can, however, say unequivocally that Bass Reeves is the closest real person to resemble the fictional Lone Ranger on the American western frontier of the nineteenth century" (Burton 14). In addition, when I questioned the validity of Burton's theory on my blog in April of 2015, the author himself commented: "In regards to Bass Reeves being the inspiration for the Lone Ranger fictional character, I never said that it was definitive, but coincidental similarities" (www.martingrams.blogspot.com).

In 2015, Bill O'Reilly's *Legends and Lies: The Real West* was published by Henry Holt and Company, LLC, featuring 12 profiles of American legends of the western frontier. The sixth chapter, "Bass Reeves," borrowed liberally from Burton's book, in an attempt to "dig deep, uncovering facts that illuminate the legends and debunk the lies that have somehow become folklore" (O'Reilly 3). What O'Reilly's book accomplished, along with the filmed documentary series of the same name, however, was the exact opposite. Page after page the career of Bass Reeves was documented with repeated comparisons to the fictional adventures of *The Lone Ranger*, culminating in paragraph form the following summary: "Did he serve as the model for *The Lone Ranger*? There is no specific evidence that he did, and the men credited with creating the character in 1933 never spoke about it" (O'Reilly 133). Yet, the accomplishments of Bass Reeves was overshadowed in the book with the suggestion that racial injustice was served upon the legendary lawman, adding fuel to a fire of controversy, and once again pushing Reeves's credible accomplishments to the sidelines.

It should also be noted that anchorman and political commentator Bill O'Reilly merely lent use of his celebrity status to the book that bore his name on the cover. As revealed within the contents of the book, David Fisher, a journalist and *New York Times* bestseller, was the author. Through Fisher's own admission he consulted Art T. Burton's *Black Gun, Silver Star* biography and three blogs found on the Internet. It should also be noted that no other books documenting the career of Bass Reeves, published in the last decade, reprinted any reference of the Lone Ranger myth.

The origin of *The Lone Ranger* radio program, on the other hand, is well documented with nothing to indicate Bass Reeves was in any way the inspiration for the fictional character. The series originated in December 1932 when George W. Trendle, owner of radio station WXYZ in Detroit, Michigan, wanted to produce a western program that would interest local sponsors. James Jewell, the dramatic director at radio station WXYZ, was ordered by Trendle to create a Western program. What was originally created for the business of selling airtime was regarded as a throwaway property. With the conclusion of each radio broadcast, the radio scripts were tossed into the garbage and the next week's production went into rehearsal. It was not until January of 1938 that *The Lone Ranger* program was transcribed (recorded) as a business decision to syndicate across the country on smaller independent radio stations. After review of the first 700 radio scripts (dated 1933 to 1937), it was verified that the character of The Lone Ranger as we know it today was not the same in 1933.

Fran Striker, a gifted writer with a penchant for recycling plots from motion-pictures and pulp fiction, supplied the printed page. As you will observe in the following paragraphs, *The Lone Ranger* was never created by a single individual. Every aspect of the legendary cowboy developed over a period of time, with multiple hands influencing various traits, most out of dramatic necessity.

Numerous books document the history of *The Lone Ranger*, most with accurate detail. Two noteworthy examples are *From Out of the Past: A Pictorial History of The Lone Ranger* by Dave Holland (Holland House, 1989) and *Wyxie Wonderland: An Unauthorized 50-Year Diary of WXYZ Detroit* by Dick Osgood (Bowling Green University Popular Press, 1981). Both Holland and Osgood interviewed actors, producers, directors and writers who were involved with *The Lone Ranger* program to gather facts and, more importantly, dug through archival documents, including letters and interoffice memos, to verify the stories relayed to each author through verbal recollection. Osgood went one step further and dug through paper archives consisting of letters, interoffice memos, telegrams, contracts and other archival materials to verify the facts before quoting the actors verbatim.

With the intention of scanning historical documents to back up these facts, I personally made a trip to the Detroit Public Library in Michigan to browse through the archives of George W. Trendle, Dick Osgood, and attorney Raymond Meurer which are housed at the Burton Historical Collection. (The name of the library collection and of author Art T. Burton are coincidental). The facts regarding the formation and creation of *The Lone Ranger* are substantiated through historical documents (complete scans found in Appendix B), which are considered by historians and scholars as positive proof of the timetable and formation of *The Lone Ranger*.

The earliest historical document for the development of *The Lone Ranger* is dated December 28, 1932, when radio director James Jewell at radio station WXYZ in Detroit, Michigan, wrote a letter asking Striker to write up "three or four wild west thrillers using as the central figure the Lone Ranger including all the hokum of the masked rider, rustlers, killer Pete, heroine on train tracks..." (Jewell, Appendix B). As a former theatre owner, Trendle knew Westerns were among the most popular movies and certainly the most profitable. Jewell created a western of his own, but it failed to impress the boss and lasted only a short time before he chose to contact Fran Striker. Striker, then a resident of Buffalo, New York, was already scripting on a regular basis a radio program titled *Warner Lester, Manhunter*, and had proven to Jewell that he was capable of meeting the strictest of deadlines.

Through a series of letters exchanged between Jewell and Striker, rough sketches and various drafts of radio scripts were submitted, changes were suggested and implemented, and finally on January 21, 1933, a letter from Jewell advised Striker that the new series would start the following Monday, January 30. The same letter made a few suggestions before concluding, "I hope the above suggestions won't cramp your style. I realize they have changed the character you have created... but only in a minor way..." (Jewell, Appendix B). The same letter from Jewell to Striker added, "Continue to use the silver bullet and silver horseshoe gag – it's good." As verified through this letter, it was Striker who created the silver bullets and silver horseshoes. The creation of the faithful Indian sidekick, however, originates with Jewell.

The character of Tonto was brought into the series beginning with episode 11 of *The Lone Ranger*. He was born out of theatrical necessity. With just the singular hero and his horse, the narrator was required to play too big a role in explaining the plotline of the episode to the listening audience. In radio plays, dialogue served the dual purpose of telling the story and describing the background of the scenes and the actions of others. In theater and television productions, audiences can see what is happening, but on radio's audio-only format, it had to be described. Jewell asked Striker to create a sidekick. On February 18, Jewell told Striker, "It might be a good idea, also, to have an Indian half-breed who always stands ready by his command to help him make his changes." In a response dated February 20, 1933, Striker wrote: "You will notice the birth of Tonto... carrying a certain mysterious background. I have tried to work into this script the suggestions you sent. By the way, the name Tonto may not be as good as some other name so if you rechristen him I'll try and catch it on the air." Fran Striker was able to pick up Michigan radio stations on certain evenings at certain hours. Whatever revisions Jewell made to the scripts during rehearsals and airtime, Striker made note to incorporate those changes into the next script.

It was commonplace for bounty hunters and U.S. marshals to hire an Indian guide when venturing into unknown territory. Art T. Burton's theory that Bass Reeves had an Indian ride along with him on at least one mission, and that The Lone Ranger had a faithful Indian scout as a sidekick, is never a strong enough coincidence to claim *The Lone Ranger* was based on the adventures of Bass Reeves.

It should also be noted that until November 1933, eight months after the premiere of *The Lone Ranger*, George W. Trendle was never aware the radio scripts were written by Fran Striker. Trendle knew of Striker's ability to churn out scripts for *Warner Lester* but he was under the false assumption that Jewell was typing the scripts himself. From December 1932 to February 1933, Jewell participated in story conferences with George W. Trendle, regarding the direction and formation of *The Lone Ranger*, then relayed that information to Striker for execution. The elements that made up the characteristics of *The Lone Ranger* were borne from pulp magazine fare. A letter from Jewell to Striker, dated January 21, verified Trendle's request for a happy-go-lucky, laugh-at-danger masked vigilante similar to *The Mark of Zorro*. Jewell provided suggestions that worked with the physical demands of daily radio drama, Striker provided the rough sketches. *The Lone Ranger* working in disguise originated from this letter as a result of Jewell's reference to *The Mark of Zorro*. It should also be noted that the radio program depicted a different type of masked vigilante than the one we are accustomed to today. Throughout 1933 and the early half of 1934, *The Lone Ranger* fool-heartedly laughed at danger just as Zorro and Robin Hood ridiculed their combatants before and after swordplay.

When Trendle learned of Striker's involvement a few days before Thanksgiving, he contacted him personally to offer a permanent job at the station in Detroit. By May of 1934, Striker accepted and months later moved his family to Detroit. It remains a flimsy argument for Art T. Burton to claim three people, one living two state borders away, to have conspired against the legendary Bass Reeves, with no reference to any true-life historical figure among all of the archival correspondence, especially since the name Bass Reeves was never featured in any published reference books prior to 1971. Moreover, multiple letters and telegrams established that fiction literature of swash-buckling fare and masked vigilantes were the true inspiration for the character.

The greatest influence on the formation of *The Lone Ranger* was Tom Mix, evident in a letter dated January 21, 1933, in which Jewell told Striker, "We are going to publicize the fact that the Ranger is a Tom Mix type." Tom Mix was a Hollywood movie star who defined the genre of Westerns during the early days of cinema. Mix was an icon young children admired and Jewell was attempting to mirror that same success story.

Through archival documents in Detroit it has been established that Trendle himself had no involvement with the formation of *The Lone Ranger* (the horse named Silver or the Indian companion named Tonto) beyond financial backing as owner and operator of the radio station, and the formal request to Jewell to create a Western program for evening programming.

The connection between Bass Reeves and the fictional *Lone Ranger* is questionable at best, in part because the author employs Transmedial Migration; i.e. the adaptation of the properties of fictional characters to real-life historical figures. Burton chose to find a connection from fiction to real-life, not the other way around as most historians would insist. For decades in colleges and universities across the country, history professors have instructed their students to avoid this pitfall. Respected historians also avoid printing theories with no facts to back up their belief, knowing that many readers mistake assumptions for fact, thus creating "false beliefs." Thus, the first chapter of Burton's book diverts attention from the admirably outlined chronicle of Reeves's accomplishments as documented in the remaining chapters. Bloggers today, however, continue to reprint the misconception that Bass Reeves was the inspiration for *The Lone Ranger*. No one has, as of today, found any historical documents to prove such a connection between the two. Yet, multiple historical documents have disproved the myth.

The principals of accuracy, fairness and truthfulness are never among editorial guidelines for Internet blogs, which instead often rely on sensationalism and controversy for search engine optimization. The Bass Reeves-*Lone Ranger* connection is a perfect example of "argumentum ad populum," Latin for "appeal to the people," an argumentation theory that concludes a proposition is true because "If many believe so, it is so" (O'Hair 122). This fallacy spreads when an argument panders to popular passion or sentiment. Statements with a shade of racial injustice are among the hot button issues on the Internet. The legitimacy of any statement should never depend on its popularity, but on its truth credentials. No better example can be found than the 2016 Presidential Election, when "Fake News" became a concern to the general public. It was then that historians and scholars were able to demonstrate the difficulty of surfing the Internet for valid news items. Michael Radutzky, a producer for television's *60 Minutes*, once said his show considered fake news to be "stories that are probably false, have enormous traction [popular appeal] in the culture, and are consumed by millions of people.") This author will not break down the numerous reasons why bloggers today feel a need to reprint what they read on other blogs, without verifying the sources, but remind readers that the validity of an author's work relies on their sources.

When once asked who created *The Lone Ranger*, Fran Striker remarked, "Only God creates." Without Trendle's financial backing, *The Lone Ranger* would never have continued beyond a few months. Without Jim Jewell's direction, the role of the fictional masked man would have gone a different direction – with or without an Indian sidekick. It was Jewell's production genius that interpreted the scripts and composed a finish product with cast and crew.

So why do people continue to reprint a myth that has no basis in truth? At its most basic level, racism is a lens through which people interpret, naturalize and reproduce inequality. The problem is that when there are no actual instances of discrimination, emotional contagion is applied – having one person's emotions and related behaviors trigger similar emotions and behaviors in other people. Blogs, along with social media, provide platforms for emotional contagion and unfounded accusations of racism. Similar to the premature announcement of a celebrity death, while the celebrity remains alive and well, readers are quick to accept an account without verifying the facts or the source. At its core, racism is a system in which another race benefits from the oppression of others. In the case of the Bass Reeves controversy, it is inconceivable the writers and producers of *The Lone Ranger* radio program could have known about the exploits of Bass Reeves, a lawman who was never recorded in history books in 1933. Thus, there is no evidence the creators of *The Lone Ranger* benefited from or oppressed the reputation of Bass Reeves. Yet, postings about *The Lone Ranger* character based on the heroic exploits of Bass Reeves galvanizes people into action.

With the origin of the myth exposed and debunked, the only solution is to squash what is often perceived as discrimination. While the real life of Bass Reeves deserves to be better-known, it is unfortunate that this fanciful "inspiration for the *Lone Ranger* character" theory is what has brought him additional attention. Bloggers would provide a good turn to Bass Reeves by documenting his accomplishments, rather than repeating a myth that diverts attention from his achievements. Hollywood producers follow an axiom among the trade that states, "If you have to choose between fact and fiction, the latter sells more tickets." While every man and woman of color would agree that Bass Reeves should be remembered for what he accomplished, the controversy surrounding his exploits and an unfounded comparison to a fictional children's program that bore no resemblance or connection to Bass Reeves will continue only so long as magazine writers and bloggers fail to investigate the facts.

**APPENDIX A**

The name of Bass Reeves appears in relatively few printed reference guides prior to Burton's book. The following is a list of these books.

*The Black West: A Documentary and Pictorial History of the African American Role in the Westward Expansion of the United States* by William Loren Katz (Broadway Publishing, 2005)

*The Western Peace Officer: A Legacy of Law and Order* by Frank Richard Prassel (University of Oklahoma Press, 1972)

*Black Indians: A Hidden Heritage* by William Loren Katz (Atheneum, 1986)

*African Americans: Voices of Triumph: Perseverance* (Time-Life Books, 1993)

*The Taming of the West: Age of the Gunfighter* by Joseph G. Rosa (Salamander Books, 1993)

*The Story of Oklahoma* by W. David Baird and Danny Goble (University of Oklahoma Press, 1994)

*Black Profiles in Courage* by Kareem Abdul-Jabbar and Alan Steinberg (William Morrow, 1996)

*Best of the West* by Bill O'Neal (Publications International, 1997)

*Zeke and Ned* by Larry McMurtry and Diana Ossana (Pocket Books 1997)

*Lawmen of the Old West: The Good Guys* by Del Cain (Republic of Texas Press, 2000)

*The Wild West: Lawmen, Outlaws, Ghost Towns and More* by Bill O'Neal, James A. Crutchfield and Dale Walker (Publications International, 2001)

*Isaac C. Parker: Frontier Justice on the Frontier* by Michael J. Brodhead (University of Oklahoma Press, 2003)

*The Encyclopedia of Lawmen, Outlaws and Gunfighters* (Checkmark Books, 2003)

# APPENDIX B
Scans of historical documents to back up the facts cited in this essay.

## KUNSKY-TRENDLE BROADCASTING CORPORATION
### EXECUTIVE OFFICES
SUITE THIRD FLOOR MADISON THEATRE BUILDING
### DETROIT

GEO. W. TRENDLE
  PRESIDENT & GEN. MANAGER
JOHN H. KUNSKY
  VICE PRESIDENT & TREASURER
HOWARD O. PIERCE
  SECRETARY & STUDIO MANAGER

STATION WXYZ
DETROIT

STATIONS WOOD AND WASH
GRAND RAPIDS

December 28th, 1932

Mr. Frans Striker
261 Lexington Avenue
Buffalo, New York

Dear Mr. Striker:

    I haven't had the time to read through the serial story you sent me, but will get at it as soon as possible. Recently I worked a little stunt that I thought you might be interested in hearing about.

    In the two episode story where Axford was shot, I changed the closing announcement to the effect that Axford, despite his jocular mood was pronounced in a critical condition by the attending surgeons and informed the radio audience that a word of encouragement might help to bring him back to the Manhunter stories. The following night I put on a 'short' with Lester and Louise pacing the corridor outside of the operating room with dialogue to the point that Axford was in a serious condition. A doctor came out of the operating room and informed Lester that he had done all that he possible could and the fate of Axford was in the hands of someone else. It was very gratifying to find the audience's reaction to this little stunt. We received twenty-three hundred pieces of mail, four bouquets of flowers and hundreds of cards of condolence. Yes, they seem to like Axford. I thought I'd pass this along as you may be able to use it for your sales.

    Will you write up three or four wild west 'thrillers' using as the central figure the Lone-Ranger including all the hookum of the masked rider, rustlers, killer Pete, heroine on train tracks, fight on top of box cars, Indian bad-mad, two gun bank robbers, etc. I have an idea that this type of thing might command a large audience among the fourteen or fifteen year old kids and if they are successful, we might alternate them with the Manhunter series, (which, no doubt, will be a relief to you).

    I would appreciate a few of these westeners as soon as possible. Try and make them complete in one episode, but if you find yourself crampt for space, extend it to two.

    Thanking you for your services in the past, I remain

Yours very truly,

James E. Jewell

# KUNSKY-TRENDLE BROADCASTING CORPORATION

EXECUTIVE OFFICES
SUITE THIRD FLOOR MADISON THEATRE BUILDING
DETROIT

GEO. W. TRENDLE
  PRESIDENT & GEN. MANAGER
JOHN H. KUNSKY
  VICE PRESIDENT & TREASURER
HOWARD O. PIERCE
  SECRETARY & STUDIO MANAGER

STATION WXYZ
DETROIT

STATIONS WOOD AND WASH
GRAND RAPIDS

January 21st, 1933

Mr. Frans Striker
261 Lexington Avenue
Buffalo, New York

Dear Friend Striker:

    I am going to start the Lone Ranger series Monday, the 30th and I am herein including the few suggestions I spoke of in my last letter. If it is humanly possible, I would like to have six more of these scripts by that time. I am going to use script No. 2 as the opening bill because I feel that it is more characteristic of the type of story we will want to use.

    I am including the opening I desire along with interludes that we would like to have along with the musical interludes. We tried it both ways and find that the narrator speeds the story up considerably and keeps the tempo.

    Regarding the character of the Ranger; I feel that we can make more of him if we keep him more as a mystery man inclosing his identity only to the audience and never to the characters in the story - ala "Mark of Zero". I think you will see my point in this. I wish you would also notice on the attached script that I have struck out all reference to killing by the Lone Ranger and also the fact that I have taken the Jessie James aspect out (I realize this is good theatre, but the bosses want the Lone Ranger more of a hero for the children to pattern after). We are going to publicize the fact that the Ranger is a Tom Mix type - always doing good, never doing wrong. I think you can surmount this obstacle by the same method I used in the closing speech of script No. 2 - having the Sherrif redeem the Ranger by his unwillingness to shoot him. Of course, this is just one method, but the same psychology can apply to any other. Continue to use the silver bullet and silver horseshoe gag - it's good.

    I hope that the above suggestions won't cramp your style. I realize that they have changed the character you have created, but only in a minor way and I am hoping that it won't be difficult to conform with the wishes of my twenty bosses.

## KUNSKY-TRENDLE BROADCASTING CORPORATION

### EXECUTIVE OFFICES
SUITE THIRD FLOOR MADISON THEATRE BUILDING

### DETROIT

GEO. W. TRENDLE
PRESIDENT & GEN. MANAGER
JOHN H. KUNSKY
VICE PRESIDENT & TREASURER
HOWARD O. PIERCE
SECRETARY & STUDIO MANAGER

STATION WXYZ
DETROIT

STATIONS WOOD AND WASH
GRAND RAPIDS

February 15, 1933

Mr. Fran Striker
281 Lexington Avenue
Buffalo, New York

Dear Fran:

    In reply to your letter, which I have neglected to answer until this time, regarding the script material sent to us, I am very pleased to see that you are sending enough material through so that I can have some choice. I am very pleased to know that my production of "The Lone Ranger" story you heard, met with your satisfaction.

    We had a strange reaction from the public on this series. They were completely sold on the "Manhunter" stories and at the beginning of the "Lone Ranger" series a little animosity was shown, but the reaction we're getting now is quite favorable, to both types of stories and I feel that "The Lone Ranger" will click just as the "Manhunters" did.

    I have just one suggestion to make regarding the Ranger stories. You are not making the character of the "Lone Ranger" mysterious enough. He mingles too freely with the rest of the crowd while he is the Lone Ranger. If you have listened in, in the past few nights you will notice the changes I have made in the script, having him play one of the characters mingling with the crowd as an individual whom everyone knows, and then making an exit, returning just as the Lone Ranger with mask etc., - then disappearing again, returning as the original character. By doing this the audience recognizes his voice and picks him out of the crowd, but they are never quite positive just who the Lone Ranger is. It might be a good idea, also, to have an Indian half-breed who always stands ready at his command to help him make his changes. I think you will see the merit of this suggestion. It adds a lot of romance and mystery to the character of the Lone Ranger.

    We are trying our damndest to sell the two series and if we do, and things pick up a bit, we will be glad to pay the $6.00 charge you mentioned. However, Fran, it's quite tough at the present time, because we are standing the whole burden of expense for the Network. If you play ball with us I am sure it will be to

**Works Cited**

"Bass Reeves." *Fort Smith National Historic Site*, 2017,

    <https://www.nps.gov/fosm/learn/historyculture/bass_reeves.htm>.

Burton, Arthur T. *Black Gun, Silver Star: The Life and Legend of Bass Reeves*.

    University of Nebraska Press, 2006.

"Frontier Lawman: Deputy U.S. Marshal Bass Reeves." *American Rifleman*, 12 February, 2015,

    <https://www.americanrifleman.org/articles/2015/2/12/frontier-lawman-deputy-us-marshal-bass-reeves/>.

Holland, Dave. *From Out of the Past: A Pictorial History of The Lone Ranger*.

    Holland House, 1989.

Klein, Donna. "Bass Reeves – Slave to American Hero." Web blog post. *Recollections*.

    Recollections, 5 Nov. 2015. Web. 4 May 2017.

O'Hair, Dan. *Real Communication: An Introduction*. Bedford/St. Martin's, 2008.

"Old West Legends: Bass Reeves, Black Hero Marshal." *Legends of America*, 2003,

    <http://www.legendsofamerica.com/we-bassreeves.html>.

O'Reilly, Bill. *Legend and Lies: The Real West*. Henry Holt and Company, LLC, 2015.

Osgood, Dick. *Wyxie Wonderland: An Unauthorized 50-Year Diary of WXYZ Detroit*.

    Bowling Green University Popular Press, 1981.

Trimble, Marshall. "U.S. Deputy Marshal Bass Reeves." Web blog post. *TrueWestMagazine*.

    True West Publishing, 10 Apr. 2015. Web. 4 May 2017.

## ABOUT THE AUTHOR

Martin Grams, Jr. is the author and co-author of more than 20 successfully published books about radio programs of the 1930s, 40s and 50s, and retro television, including *The Twilight Zone: Unlocking the Door to a Television Classic* and *The Shadow: The History and Mystery of the Radio Program, 1930-1954*. Along with co-author Terry Salomonson, Martin's credits include another of George W. Trendle's properties, *The Green Hornet: A History of Radio, Motion-Pictures, Comics and Television*, an 800-page book documenting the history of the great nephew of *The Lone Ranger*.

Martin Grams, Jr. and Terry Salomonson have been hard at work finishing the first of four books documenting *The Lone Ranger*. The first is scheduled for release in the summer of 2019, tentatively titled *The Lone Ranger: The Early Years, 1933-1937*.

Made in the USA
Middletown, DE
21 May 2020